Gooseberry Patch

sandwiches

Classics

Too few people understand a
really good sandwich.
– James Beard

Sunday Morning Sandwiches

6 sandwich buns	6 eggs, beaten
1/2 c. butter, divided	1 to 2 T. Greek seasoning
1 onion, chopped	6 slices American cheese
4-oz. can sliced mushrooms, drained and divided	

Lightly coat the cut side of each bun with 1-1/2 teaspoons butter per side; brown on a griddle and set aside. Sauté onion and half the mushrooms in a 12" skillet in remining butter until golden; set aside remaining mushrooms for use in another recipe. Pour eggs on top; sprinkle with Greek seasoning to taste. When eggs begin to set; slice into 6 wedges. Flip and heat uncooked side until golden; place one slice cheese on each wedge. Serve on sandwich buns. Makes 6.

Take 'em along! Wrap each Sunday Morning Sandwich individually in wax paper or plastic wrap and they're ready for an early morning picnic or outside brunch.

Hot Ham & Cheese Sandwiches

1/2 c. butter, softened
1/2 c. onion, chopped
1-1/2 T. mustard
1-1/2 T. poppy seed

12 sandwich buns
12 slices cooked ham
12 slices Swiss cheese

Blend butter, onion, mustard and poppy seed together; spread thickly on both halves of each sandwich bun. Layer a slice of ham and cheese on each bottom bun; replace top bun. Wrap each sandwich in aluminum foil; bake at 350 degrees for 15 minutes. Makes 12.

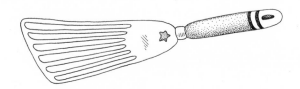

Cheddar & Bacon Breakfast Sandwiches

3 eggs, beaten
1/4 c. milk
2 T. butter
8 thick slices bread

12 slices Cheddar cheese
1/2 T. chopped walnuts
4 slices bacon, crisply cooked
    and crumbled

Whisk eggs and milk together; set aside. Melt butter over low heat on a griddle. Dip one side of each bread slice in egg mixture; lay 4 slices with coated side down on griddle. Top each with 3 cheese slices; sprinkle equally with chopped walnuts and bacon. Place remaining bread slices on top with coated side up. Heat both sides until cheese melts and bread is golden, about 5 minutes per side. Makes 4.

Italian Sausage Sandwiches

8 Italian sausages
1 sweet onion, chopped
2 green peppers, sliced
1 t. salt
1 t. sugar
1 t. Italian seasoning

2 tomatoes, chopped
8 hoagie rolls, split
4 t. butter, divided
16-oz. pkg. shredded
   mozzarella cheese,
   divided

Score the sausages every 1/2 inch; brown in a skillet for
15 minutes or until cooked through. Set aside; drain skillet,
reserving 3 tablespoons drippings. Sauté onion in reserved
drippings in same skillet until soft; add peppers, salt, sugar,
and Italian seasoning. Cover and heat for 5 minutes. Stir in
tomatoes; arrange sausages on top. Simmer, covered, for
5 minutes. Scoop out shallow centers in the bottom and tops of
the hoagie buns; spread evenly with butter. Arrange on a
baking sheet; bake at 350 degrees for 10 minutes. Divide and
sprinkle mozzarella cheese in the bottom of each hoagie bun;
place a sausage on top. Spoon desired amount sauce over the
sausages; replace top hoagie bun. Serve warm. Makes 8.

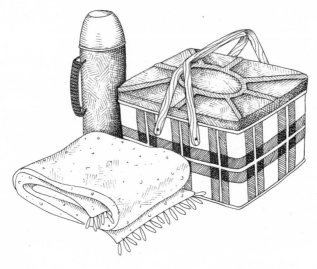

Layered Italian Sandwiches

1-lb. pkg. frozen bread
   dough, thawed
1/4 lb. salami, thinly sliced
1/4 lb. genoa ham, thinly
   sliced
1/4 lb. provolone cheese,
   thinly sliced

2-oz. pkg. pepperoni slices
8-oz. pkg. sliced mushrooms
1 green pepper, sliced into
   rings

Place dough on an aluminum foil-lined baking sheet; press into a 13"x10" rectangle. Layer center with salami, ham, provolone and pepperoni; arrange mushrooms and green pepper on top. Fold dough over filling; pinch edges to seal. Place seam side-down on a baking sheet; set aside to rise until double in bulk. Bake at 350 degrees for 45 minutes. Serves 8.

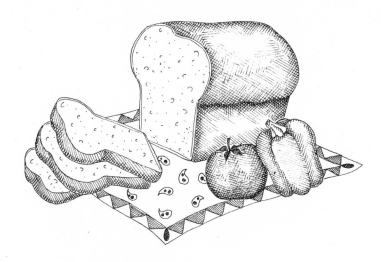

Make two of these hearty sandwiches and feed the whole team...wrap each loaf in foil to keep them warm!

Reuben Sandwich

2 slices corned beef
1 slice Swiss cheese
2 slices pumpernickel bread
4 T. sauerkraut

1-1/2 T. Thousand Island
    salad dressing
3 T. butter

Place one slice corned beef and cheese on a slice of bread. Spread sauerkraut on top of cheese; top with dressing. Add another slice of corned beef and remaining bread slice. Melt butter in a skillet over medium heat; grill both sides of sandwich until cheese is melted. Makes one sandwich.

Make 'em mini Reubens! Cut cheese and corned beef into four squares and serve on party rye slices. Instead of grilling, broil open-faced until the cheese is melted.

Friday Night Sandwiches

6-oz. can crabmeat
2 stalks celery, finely
    chopped
2 green onions, finely
    chopped
4-oz. can sliced mushrooms,
    drained

1 t. caraway seed
1-1/2 T. mayonnaise
1-1/2 T. sour cream
4 slices bread, toasted
8 slices bacon, crisply cooked
4 slices Swiss cheese

Mix first 7 ingredients together; spread evenly over bread slices. Add bacon and cheese slices; broil until cheese melts. Makes 4 servings.

Deli Skillet Sandwiches

4 oz. cooked ham, thinly
    sliced
4 oz. provolone cheese,
    thinly sliced
4 oz. cooked turkey, thinly
    sliced

8 slices rye bread
1/2 c. milk
2 eggs

Layer ham, cheese and turkey slices equally on 4 slices of bread. Top with remaining bread slices; slice each sandwich in half, diagonally and set aside. Blend eggs and milk together in a 9" pie plate; coat both sides of sandwich wedges in egg mixture. Heat both sides in a greased skillet over medium heat until golden. Arrange on a baking sheet; bake at 400 degrees for 3 to 5 minutes or until cheese melts. Makes 4.

Shredded Chicken Sandwiches

1 T. butter
1 onion, diced
1 stalk celery, chopped
1 c. chicken broth, divided
3 boneless, skinless chicken
    breasts

1 T. cornstarch
1/2 c. milk
salt and pepper to taste
6 sandwich buns

Melt butter in a saucepan; sauté onion, celery and one tablespoon chicken broth for 5 minutes. Add chicken and remaining broth; boil. Reduce heat and simmer until chicken is tender. Remove chicken; set aside to cool until it's easily handled. Shred chicken; return to saucepan until simmering. Whisk cornstarch and milk together in a small bowl; slowly stir into chicken mixture. Simmer and stir chicken until mixture is thickened but still moist, about 8 minutes. Season with salt and pepper. Spoon onto sandwich buns to serve. Makes 6.

Kept warm in a slow cooker, shredded chicken is a potluck classic! Double the batch and take it along to the next church social for a guaranteed crowd pleaser.

Pulled Pork Sandwiches

2 2-1/2 lb. boneless pork
   loins
1 c. water
2 t. salt
2 c. catsup
2 c. celery, diced

1/3 c. steak sauce
1/3 c. brown sugar, packed
1/4 c. vinegar
3 t. lemon juice
12 sandwich buns

Place roasts in an 8-quart Dutch oven; add water and salt.
Heat on medium heat for 2-1/2 hours or until meat is tender
and registers 160 degrees on a meat thermometer. Remove
roasts; shred with a fork and set aside. Skim fat from cooking
liquid and discard. Drain all but one cup cooking liquid; stir in
shredded meat and remaining ingredients except for sandwich
buns. Cover; simmer over medium heat for 1-1/2 hours. Spoon
onto sandwich buns to serve. Makes 12 servings.

Heat lemons in the microwave for 30 seconds for twice
the juice...perfect for this sandwich and
fresh-squeezed lemonade too!

Open-Faced Sandwiches

1 lb. ground beef, browned
1 onion, chopped
1 lb. bacon, crisply cooked
    and crumbled

10-3/4 oz. can tomato soup
1 c. pasteurized process
    cheese spread, cubed
8 sandwich buns

Combine all ingredients except sandwich buns in a large mixing bowl; spoon onto tops and bottoms of sandwich buns. Place on an ungreased baking sheet; bake at 400 degrees for 10 minutes. Makes 16.

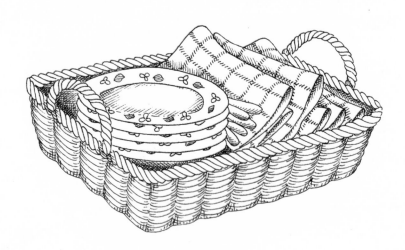

Place just a corner of a bread slice between your teeth while cutting onions and your eyes won't water!

Over-Stuffed Pockets

3 whole pitas, cut in half
lettuce leaves
6 thin slices deli ham
6 slices Cheddar cheese
1 sweet onion, sliced into
    rings

1 tomato, sliced
ranch-style salad dressing
4 slices bacon, crisply cooked
    and crumbled

Fill pita halves with lettuce, ham, cheese, onion and tomato slices; top with ranch dressing and crumbled bacon. Makes 6.

Poor-Boy Sandwiches

1 loaf French bread
1/2 c. mayonnaise
1 c. shredded lettuce

6 thin slices roast beef
1/2 c. beef gravy, warmed
2 tomatoes, sliced

Split bread lengthwise; warm in the oven. Remove from oven; spread bottom slice with mayonnaise. Layer with lettuce and roast beef; spoon gravy over meat. Top with tomatoes; replace top half of bread. Cut into 2 or 3 slices; serve warm. Serves 2 or 3.

The fillings of Poor-Boy Sandwiches vary from region to region. In New Orleans, the fillings begin with fried potatoes and end with crabmeat...try it with your family's favorite fillings!

Best-Ever Grilled Cheese Sandwich

1/2 t. Dijon mustard	1 slice Cheddar cheese
1 T. mayonnaise	1 slice sweet onion
2 thick slices sourdough	1 to 2 slices tomato
bread	3 slices bacon, crisply cooked
1 slice Swiss cheese	butter

Mix mustard and mayonnaise together; spread on one slice of bread. Top with cheeses, onion, tomato, bacon and remaining bread slice. Spread butter on outer sides of bread. Grill on a buttered grill or skillet on both sides over low heat until cheese melts and bread is golden. Makes one sandwich.

More fun fillings for grilled cheese sandwiches! Sprinkle Parmesan cheese, Italian or Cajun seasonings, chives or even a tiny spoonful of salsa...just grill as usual.

California BLT's

1/4 c. mayonnaise-type
   salad dressing
1 T. fresh parsley, chopped
1 T. green onion, chopped
8 slices bread, toasted

4 leaves lettuce
8 slices pepper bacon, crisply
   cooked
12 slices tomato
1 avocado, peeled and sliced

Blend salad dressing, parsley and green onion together; evenly spread on 4 bread slices. Layer each with lettuce, 2 bacon slices, 3 tomato slices and a slice of avocado; top with remaining bread slices. Makes 4 sandwiches.

Pack a container of frozen lemonade or iced tea with lunch in the morning to keep everything cool. When lunchtime rolls around, enjoy a crisp sandwich and a frosty drink too!

BBQ Meat Loaf Sandwiches

1 c. barbecue sauce
1 T. cider vinegar
1 t. pepper

2-lb. meat loaf, cooked
8 onion sandwich rolls
1 c. creamy coleslaw

Combine barbecue sauce, vinegar and pepper; mix well and set aside. Cut meat loaf into 16 slices; place 2 slices on bottom half of each roll. Top with 2 tablespoons of sauce and 2 tablespoons of coleslaw; top with remaining roll half. Makes 8 servings.

Barbecue Sauce

1 onion, chopped
2 T. butter
4 T. lemon juice
3 T. Worcestershire sauce

2 T. brown sugar, packed
1 c. catsup
1 c. water
salt and pepper to taste

Combine all ingredients in a medium saucepan; simmer for 30 to 40 minutes. Makes 2-1/2 cups.

Your favorite meat loaf won't stick to the bottom of the pan when you place a slice of bacon in the bottom of the pan first. How clever!

BBQ Beef Sandwiches

5 T. brown sugar, packed
   and divided
3/4 t. pepper
2 1-lb. flank steaks
1 c. onion, chopped
1 c. tomato paste
3 T. Worcestershire sauce
1 T. molasses

3 T. cider vinegar
1 T. chili powder
1 t. garlic powder
1 t. dry mustard
1 t. cumin
1/2 t. salt
10 submarine rolls

Combine one tablespoon brown sugar and pepper; rub onto
both sides of steaks and set aside. Stir remaining ingredients
together, except for the rolls, in a slow cooker; add steaks,
turning to coat. Cover and heat on high setting for one hour;
reduce heat to low and cook for 7 hours. Remove steaks;
reserve sauce. Shred steaks with 2 forks; return meat to slow
cooker. Stir meat and sauce together; spoon onto rolls to serve.
Makes 10 servings.

Choose one night a week to prepare dishes specific to a
region of our great country. Try BBQ Beef Sandwiches
with a side of coleslaw for a down-home southern dinner!

Chicken-Cheddar Wraps

1 c. sour cream
1 c. salsa
2 T. mayonnaise
4 c. cooked chicken, cubed
2 c. shredded Cheddar cheese

1 c. sliced mushrooms
2 c. shredded lettuce
12 flour tortillas
1 c. guacamole
Garnish: tomato wedges

Combine sour cream, salsa and mayonnaise; add chicken, cheese and mushrooms. Divide lettuce between tortillas; top with 1/4 cup chicken mixture on each tortilla. Spread with guacamole; roll up tortilla. Place tortillas on a serving dish; garnish with any remaining guacamole and tomato wedges. Makes 12 servings.

For the softest tortillas, wrap them in a damp paper towel
and microwave for about 15 seconds.
No more tearing!

Green Chile-Chicken Sandwiches

4 boneless, skinless chicken
   breasts
2/3 c. soy sauce
1/4 c. cider vinegar
2 T. sugar
2 t. oil

4-oz. can whole green chiles,
   drained and sliced
   lengthwise
4 slices Pepper Jack cheese
4 Kaiser rolls, split

Flatten chicken breasts; place into a resealable plastic bag. Combine soy sauce, vinegar, sugar and oil in a mixing bowl; set aside 1/4 cup. Pour remaining marinade over chicken; seal bag and turn to coat. Refrigerate for 30 minutes; drain and discard marinade. Grill chicken, uncovered, over medium heat for 3 minutes. Turn and baste with reserved marinade; grill 3 minutes longer or until juices run clear when pierced with a fork. Top each breast with one green chile and cheese slice; cover and grill for 2 more minutes or until cheese is melted. Serve on rolls. Makes 4 servings.

Flatten chicken between wax paper using a rolling pin and a little muscle... just throw away the paper and there's no mess!

Baked Chicken Sandwiches

4 c. chicken, cooked and
    diced
10-3/4 oz. can cream of
    mushroom soup
10-3/4 oz. can cream of
    chicken soup
3 T. onion, diced
8-oz. can whole water
    chestnuts, thinly sliced

1 loaf bread
2 eggs
1 T. milk
6 to 8 c. potato chips,
    crushed
10-1/2 oz. can chicken
    gravy, warmed

Combine chicken, soups, onion and water chestnuts together;
spread mixture on bread slices and top with another slice of
bread. Wrap in freezer paper; freeze. When ready to serve,
blend eggs and milk together; dip sandwiches. Roll in crushed
potato chips; arrange in a 13"x9" baking dish. Bake at
325 degrees for 45 minutes. Place on serving plates; pour
warm gravy on top. Makes 15 servings.

Crunch up potato chips in a hurry! Place them in a large
plastic zipping bag and roll them into crumbs with a
rolling pin...they'll be ready in no time.

Beef Stroganoff Sandwiches

2 lbs. ground beef	4 T. margarine
1/2 c. onion, chopped	2 c. sour cream
1 t. salt	2 tomatoes, sliced
1/2 t. garlic salt	1 green pepper, sliced
1/4 t. pepper	3 c. shredded Cheddar cheese
1 loaf French bread	

Brown ground beef and onion; drain. Add salt, garlic salt and pepper; set aside. Cut bread in half horizontally; spread margarine evenly on both sides and place on baking sheets. Stir sour cream into meat mixture; spoon onto bread. Layer tomatoes and green peppers over the top. Bake at 350 degrees for 10 minutes; remove from oven and sprinkle with cheese. Bake 10 more minutes or until cheese is melted. Makes 6 to 8 servings.

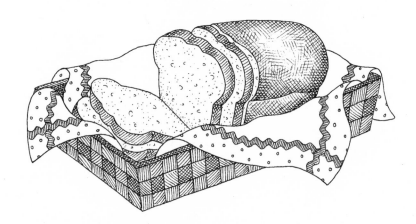

For a spicy twist on Beef Stroganoff Sandwiches,
try using herbed Italian bread instead.
Just bake as usual...yum!

Cucumber Sandwiches

8-oz. pkg. cream cheese,
    softened
1 c. mayonnaise
1-oz. pkg. dry Italian salad
    dressing mix

1 loaf party rye bread slices
1 cucumber, thinly sliced
dill weed to taste

Blend cream cheese, mayonnaise and dressing mix together in a medium mixing bowl; spread over half the bread slices. Top with a cucumber slice; sprinkle with dill weed. Arrange bread slice on top; chill until firm. Makes 40 to 50.

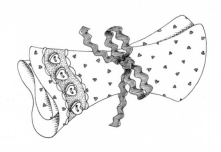

Salmon & Cream Cheese Sandwiches

1/4 lb. smoked salmon,
    thinly sliced
4 oz. cream cheese, softened

1 T. fresh dill, minced, plus
    dill sprigs for garnish
8 slices pumpernickel bread

Combine salmon, cream cheese and dill; set aside. Remove crusts from bread; spread salmon mixture evenly on top. Slice each into quarters; garnish with tiny sprigs of fresh dill. Makes 32.

Watercress & Cream Cheese Sandwiches

1/3 c. watercress
1/4 c. fresh parsley
8-oz. pkg. cream cheese,
    softened

1/4 c. butter, softened
2 T. fresh chives, chopped
salt and pepper to taste
8 slices white bread

Chop watercress and parsley together in a food processor; add cream cheese, butter, chives, salt and pepper. Blend well. Spread mixture evenly over 4 bread slices; top with remaining slices. Slice each into quarters or triangles; refrigerate until serving. Serves 4.

Store fresh parsley in the fridge upright in a glass...wrap
the stems in a dampened paper towel to keep it
fresh for up to a week!

Stuffed Turkey Salad Sandwiches

3 c. turkey, cooked and
   shredded
1/2 c. mayonnaise-type
   salad dressing
1/4 c. onion, chopped
1/8 c. celery, chopped

1/8 c. water chestnuts,
   chopped
1/4 c. dried cranberries
1/4 c. chopped nuts
12 dinner rolls

Mix all ingredients together except dinner rolls; set aside. Slice
and remove tops of dinner rolls; scoop out centers. Fill rolls
with turkey mixture; replace tops. Makes 12 servings.

Celebrating at a 4th of July picnic? Take these
sandwiches along in a picnic basket and toss in a
few mini flags and sparklers too!

Tuna-Egg Salad Sandwiches

4 eggs, hard-boiled peeled
   and chopped
6-oz. can tuna, drained
2 T. sweet onion, minced
3 T. mayonnaise-type salad
   dressing

2 T. honey mustard
salt and pepper to taste
10 slices bread
5 leaves lettuce
5 slices tomato
1-1/4 c. alfalfa sprouts

Blend eggs, tuna, onion, salad dressing, mustard, salt and pepper together; divide and spread equally over 5 bread slices. Layer each with lettuce leaf, tomato slice and 1/4 cup alfalfa sprouts; top with remaining bread slices. Slice diagonally to serve. Serves 5.

Quilt sandwiches! Spread a favorite sandwich filling on different types of bread...white, rye, pumpernickel and sourdough. Slice each sandwich into quarters then mix & match each quarter on a serving platter.

Savory Tomato-Basil Tea Sandwiches

butter
mayonnaise
1 loaf party rye bread slices
1 pt. cherry tomatoes, sliced

salt
cracked peppercorns
1/3 c. fresh basil, chopped

Spread butter and then mayonnaise on one side of each slice of bread. Top with one or two tomato slices; sprinkle with salt, pepper and basil. Refrigerate until chilled. Serves 8.

Combine this simple pesto with butter or mayo to spice up
these Savory Tomato-Basil Tea Sandwiches. Place
2 cloves garlic, one cup fresh basil, 1/3 cup olive oil,
salt and pepper to taste in a food processor and
blend until a coarse paste forms. Combine
with butter or mayo for a tasty spread!

Cobb Sandwich

2 T. blue cheese salad
    dressing
3 slices bread, toasted
4-oz. pkg. boneless, skinless
    chicken breasts, grilled

1 leaf lettuce
2 slices tomato
3 slices avocado
1 slice sweet onion
3 slices bacon, crisply cooked

Spread blue cheese dressing on one side of each slice of toasted bread. On the first slice of bread, place chicken breast on dressing; top with a second bread slice. Layer on lettuce, tomato, avocado, onion and bacon; top with remaining bread slice. Cut sandwich into quarters; secure each section with a toothpick. Makes one sandwich.

Enjoy Cobb Sandwiches outside on cool summer
evenings...add a few votives to the picnic table and,
afterward, enjoy the fireflies and starlight.

Club Sandwich

1/2 c. mayonnaise
1-1/2 t. fresh parsley,
   minced
1 t. green onion, minced
1 t. sweet pickle, minced
2 t. vinegar

3 slices bread, toasted
4 thin slices cooked chicken
3 slices tomato
3 slices bacon, crisply cooked
salt and pepper to taste

Blend first 5 ingredients together in a small mixing bowl; cover
and refrigerate until chilled. When serving, spread evenly on
one side of each piece of toast; add chicken, another bread
slice, tomato slices and bacon. Season with salt and pepper.
Top with remaining toast slice; cut into quarters diagonally to
serve, using a toothpick to hold together. Makes one sandwich.

Make ordinary sandwiches extraordinary! Look for picks
usually used to decorate cupcakes at party supply
stores...they'll look charming in this Club Sandwich too.

Chicken Salad Sandwiches

6 boneless, skinless chicken breasts, cooked and cubed
1 T. fresh parsley, chopped
1 t. fresh dill, chopped
2 T. green pepper, chopped
2 T. celery, chopped
1/3 c. carrots, chopped
2/3 c. chopped walnuts
1 t. pepper
mayonnaise to taste
salt to taste
6 to 8 sandwich buns

Place chicken, parsley, dill, green pepper, celery, carrots, walnuts and pepper in a medium mixing bowl. Stir in enough mayonnaise to achieve desired spreading consistency; salt to taste. Spoon onto buns to serve. Serves 6 to 8.

Spoon homemade chicken salad onto toasted sandwich buns, into hearty pita pockets or stuff inside a fresh-picked tomato...it's delicious no matter how it's served!

Rose Petal Sandwiches

8-oz. pkg. cream cheese,
   softened
3 T. rose water
12 thin slices white bread,
   crusts trimmed

6 unsprayed red or pink
   roses, petals only

Blend cream cheese and rose water together; spread equally onto bread slices. Cover each slice with rose petals; press gently into cream cheese. Cover; refrigerate until firm. Slice into halves and then slice each half into quarters. Makes 3 to 4 dozen servings.

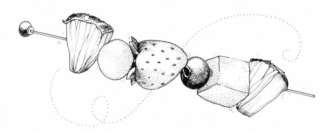

Tropical Sandwiches

8-oz. pkg. strawberry cream
   cheese, softened
10 slices pound cake
10 strawberries, hulled and
   sliced

3 bananas, peeled and sliced
seedless grapes, sliced in
   half

Spread cream cheese evenly over pound cake slices; layer equally with fruit slices, pressing gently into cream cheese layer. Makes 10.

Deluxe Ice Cream Sandwiches

1-1/2 c. butter
3 c. long-cooking oats,
  uncooked
1-1/2 T. all-purpose flour
1 t. salt
1-3/4 c. sugar

2 t. vanilla extract
2 eggs, lightly beaten
1/2 gal. vanilla ice cream,
  softened
jimmies

Melt butter in a large saucepan over low heat; cool. Add oats, flour, salt, sugar and vanilla; stir to combine. Mix in eggs; blend well. Spoon 1-1/2 tablespoons batter onto a buttered, parchment-covered baking sheet; allow at least 3 inches per cookie. Flatten batter into circles; bake at 350 degrees for 15 minutes. Set aside to cool. Spread flat side of one cookie with ice cream to one-inch thickness; lay another cookie on top, flat side-down. Roll edges of ice cream in jimmies; place into freezer until firm. Repeat with remaining cookies. Makes 2 dozen.

Use cookie cutters to make whimsical ice cream sandwiches. Cut out cookies and slices of ice cream, stack and freeze for a frosty treat anytime.

Just copy and cut out this
recipe card...kids can color
and then fill it out with
their favorite fillings!

My favorite sandwich

Make a lunch time wish!
Label with the kind of
sandwich, the recipient's name and
write a special note inside!

Index